Montessori Addition Operation Workbook

2

Montessori Math
Addition Operation
Activities for Grade 2
in One Book!

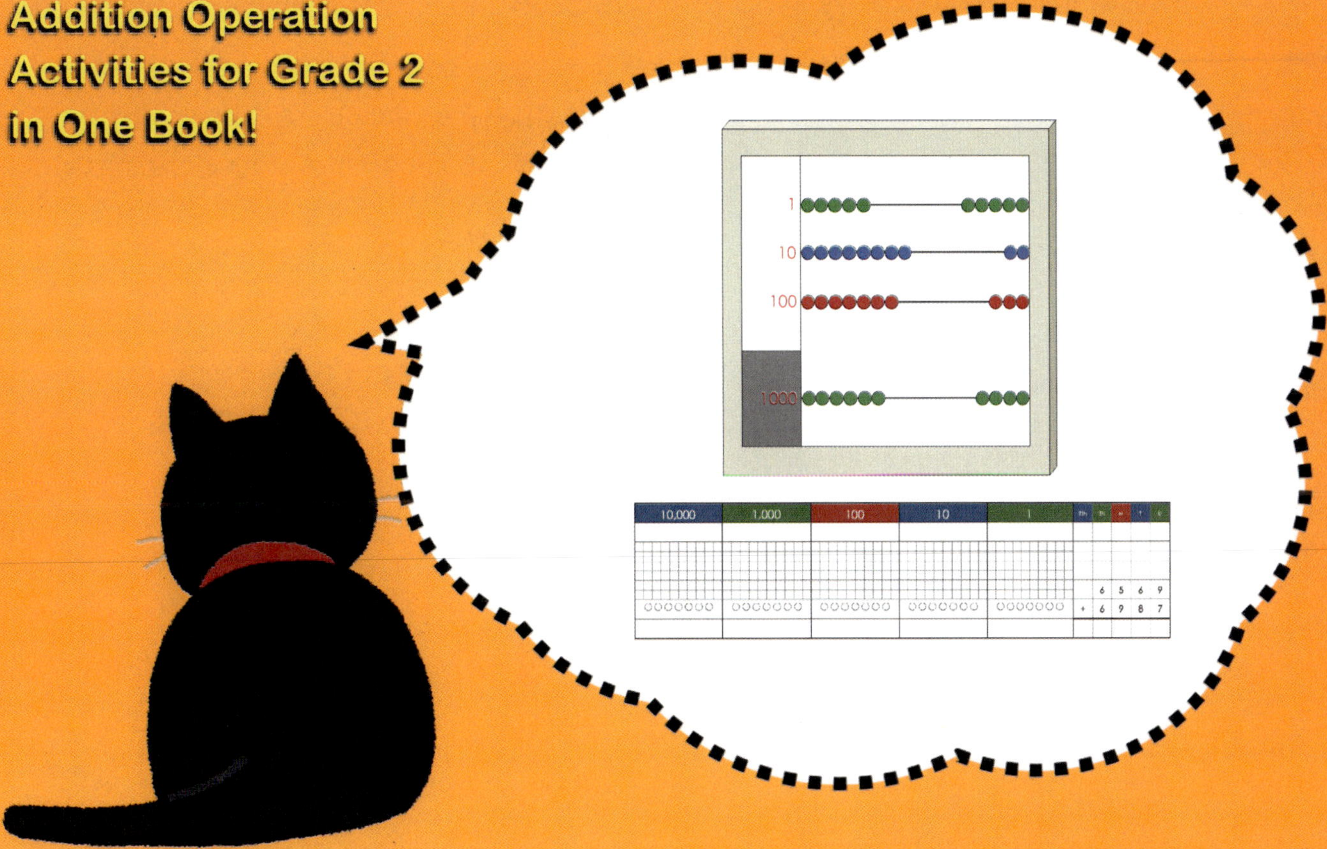

By Ayako Thiessen
Meowntessori Montessori
www.meowntessori.com

INDEX

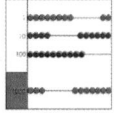 **Dot Game**

Page **1** Addition

Small Bead Frame

Page **9** Introduction

Page **17** Static Addition

Page **25** Dynamic Addition

Meowntessori Montessori

Printable Materials / Workbooks / Worksheets

Dot Game

Addition
Workbook

www.meowntessori.com

© Meowntessori Montessori All Rights Reserved

How to Use

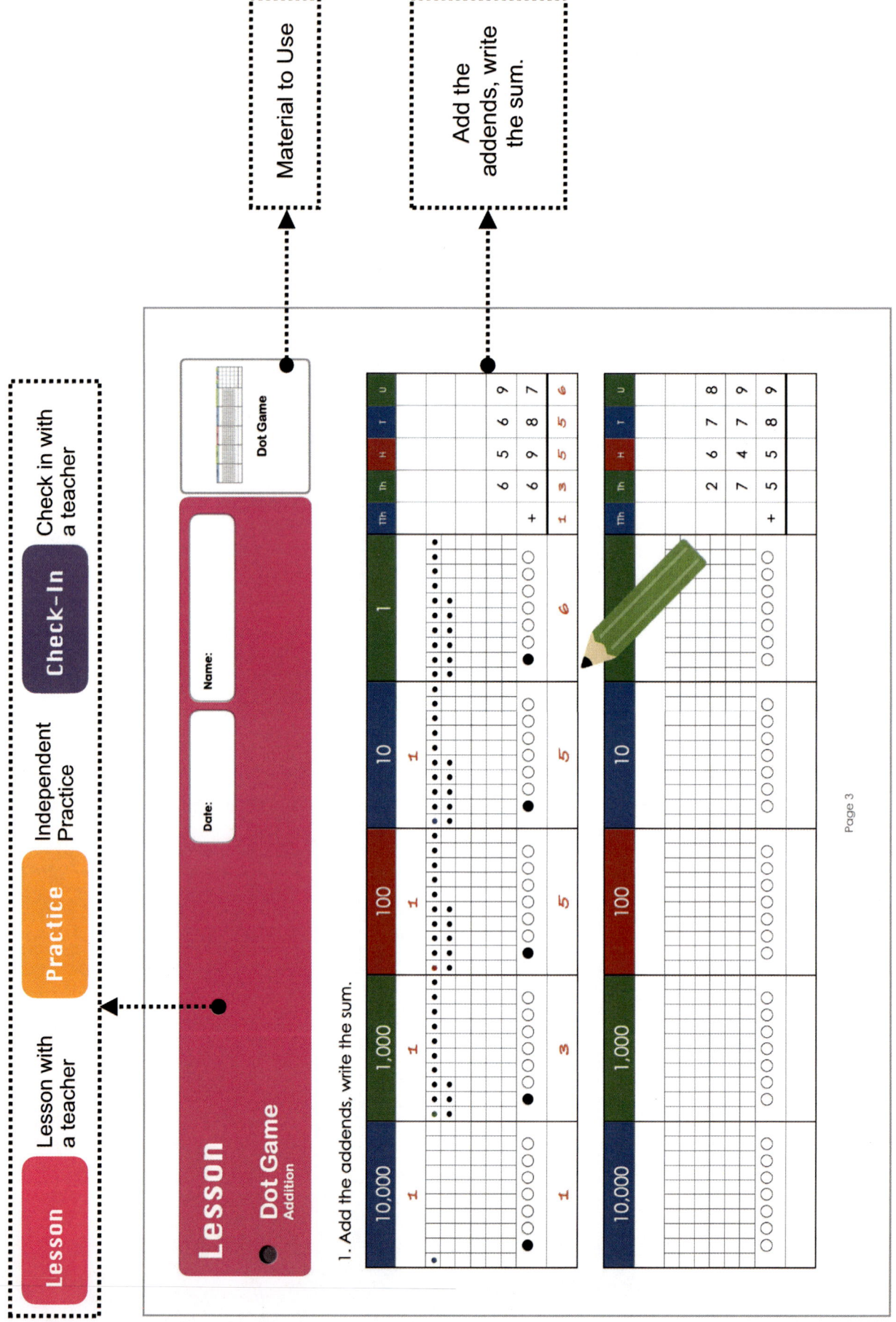

Lesson

Dot Game
Addition

Name:

Date:

1. Add the addends, write the sum.

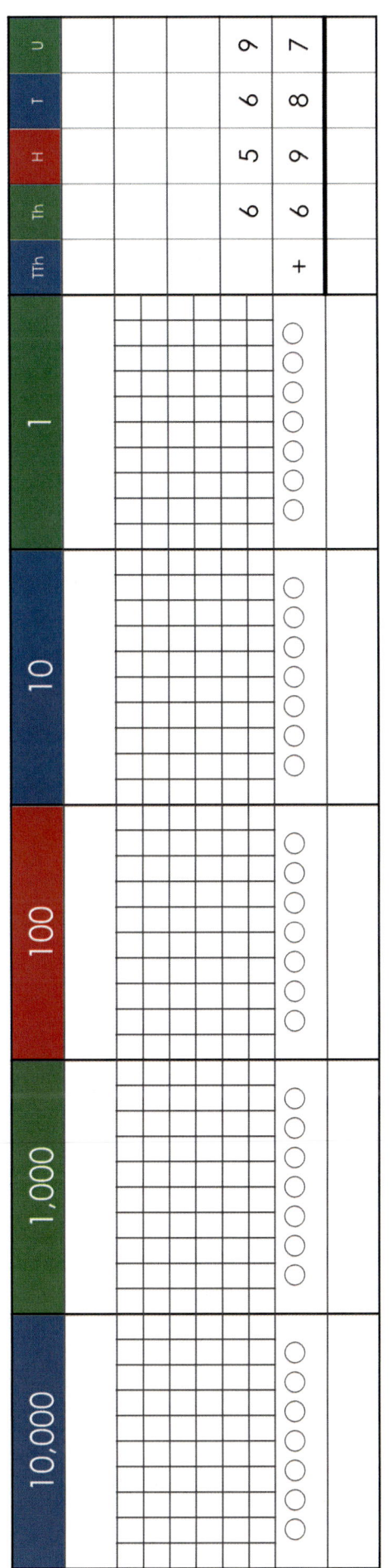

Practice 1

Dot Game
Addition

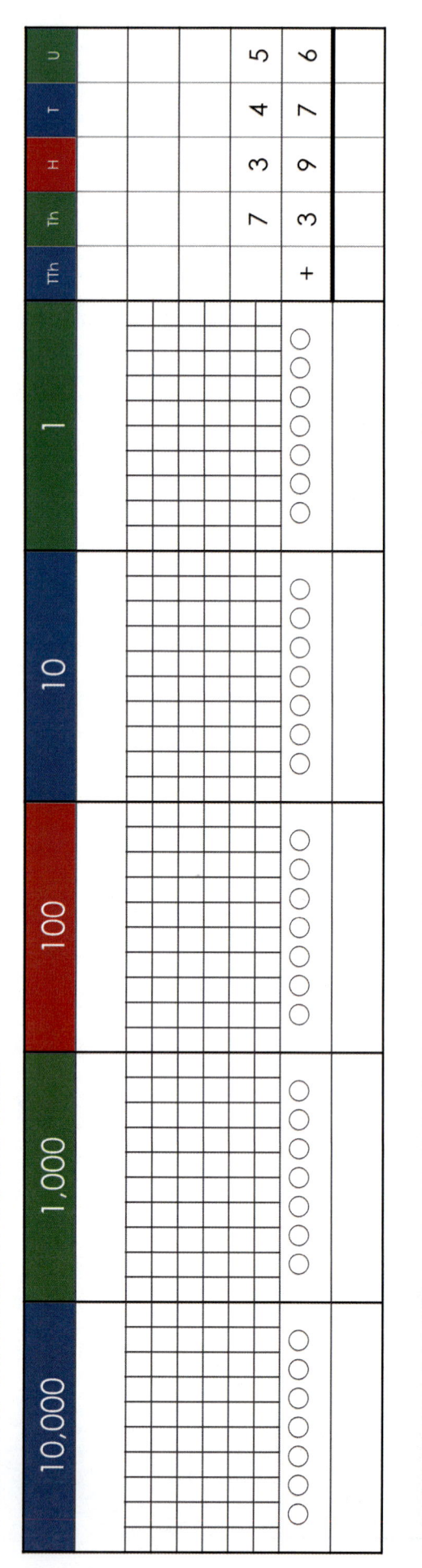

Name:

Date:

1. Add the addends, write the sum.

TTh	Th	H	T	U
	7	3	4	5
+	3	9	7	6

TTh	Th	H	T	U
	5	8	9	4
	6	7	8	6
+	8	9	4	9

Page 4

Practice 2

Dot Game
Addition

Name:

Date:

1. Add the addends, write the sum.

TTh	Th	H	T	U
	4	6	7	3
	6	9	3	7
	7	3	8	9
+	3	7	6	5

TTh	Th	H	T	U
	8	7	3	2
	2	9	9	8
	1	4	6	4
+	5	7	7	9

Page 5

Practice 3

Dot Game
Addition

Name:

Date:

1. Add the addends, write the sum.

TTh	Th	H	T	U
	5	9	7	3
	6	8	4	5
	7	7	2	8
	8	6	1	9
+	2	4	7	4

TTh	Th	H	T	U
	6	6	9	5
	3	9	4	7
	7	5	3	1
	5	6	7	3
+	2	7	4	9

Practice 4

Dot Game
Addition

Name:

Date:

1. Add the addends, write the sum.

TTh	Th	H	T	U
	4	9	3	6
	6	8	6	5
	3	3	5	4
	8	8	8	7
+	1	7	2	1

TTh	Th	H	T	U
	5	8	6	9
	4	3	7	2
	9	9	5	3
	9	8	8	6
+	1	5	3	4

Page 7

Check-in

Date:

Name:

Dot Game

Dot Game
Addition

1. Add the addends, write the sum.

10,000	1,000	100	10	1	TTh	Th	H	T	U
						6	7	9	6
						4	6	9	5
						8	4	9	3
						6	5	4	7
					+	1	2	9	2

10,000	1,000	100	10	1	TTh	Th	H	T	U
						3	4	4	9
						9	7	8	3
						8	3	5	2
						7	9	4	5
					+	6	2	3	3

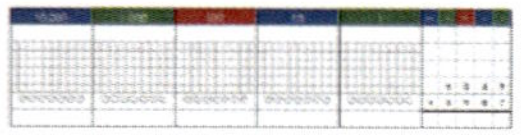

Meowntessori Montessori
Printable Materials / Workbooks / Worksheets

Small Bead Frame

Introduction

Workbook

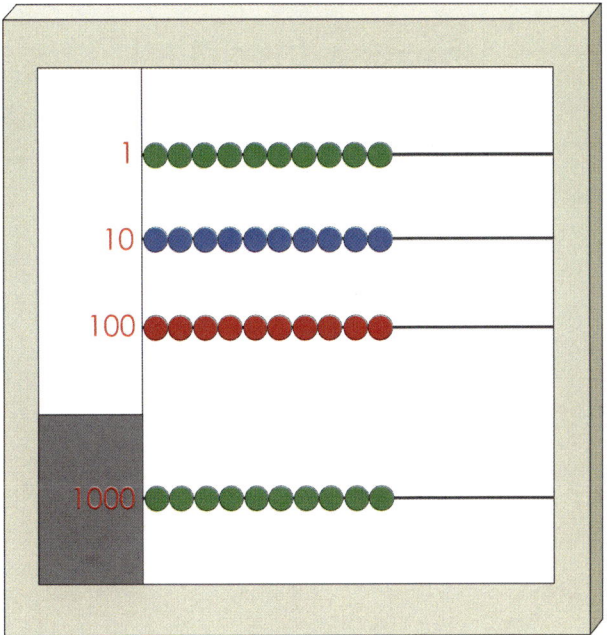

www.meowntessori.com

© Meowntessori Montessori All Rights Reserved

How to work

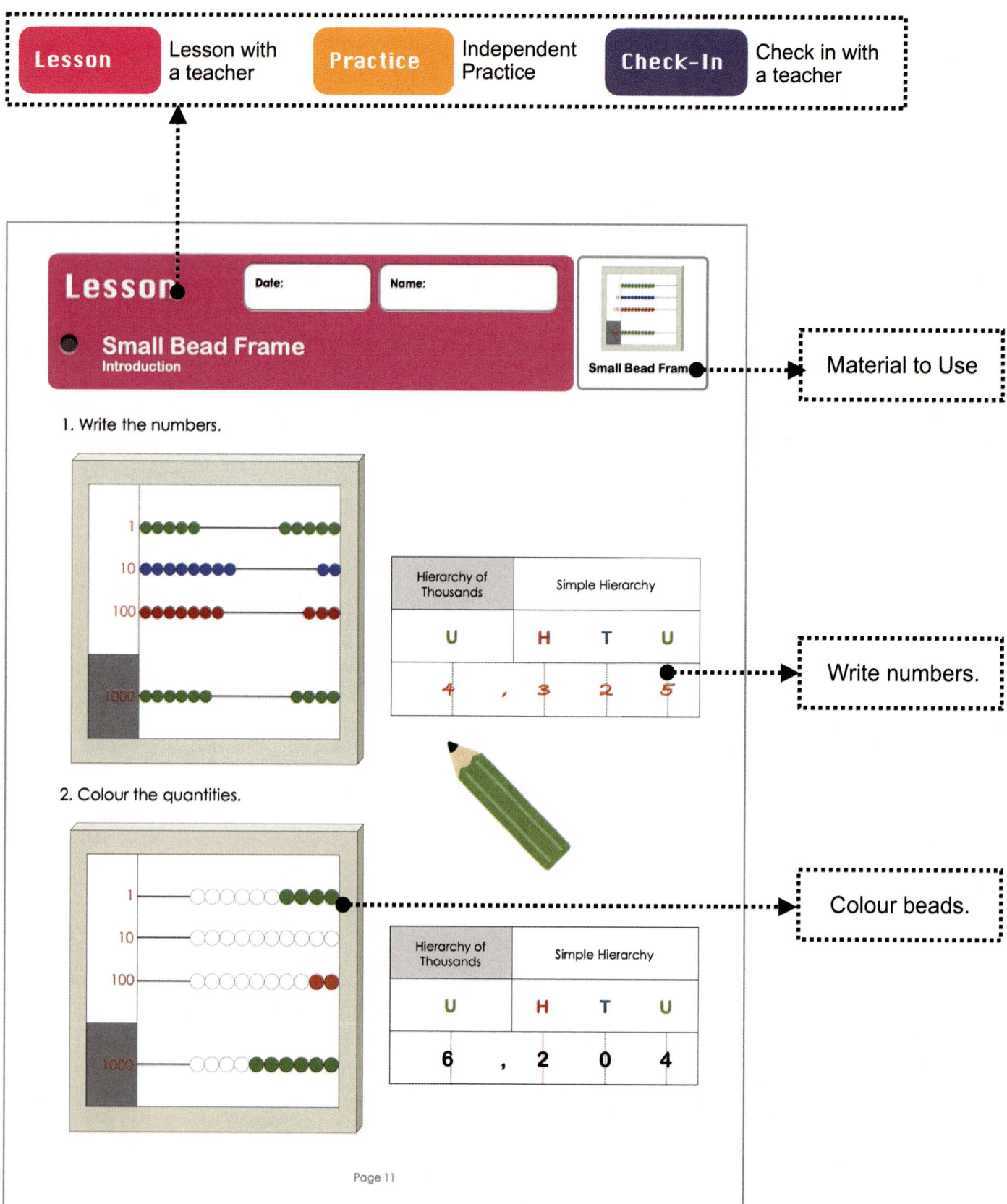

Lesson

Small Bead Frame
Introduction

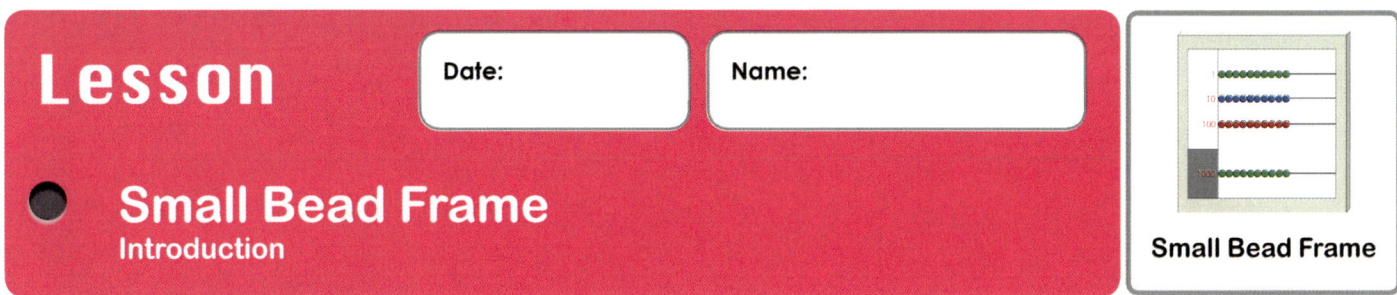

1. Write the numbers.

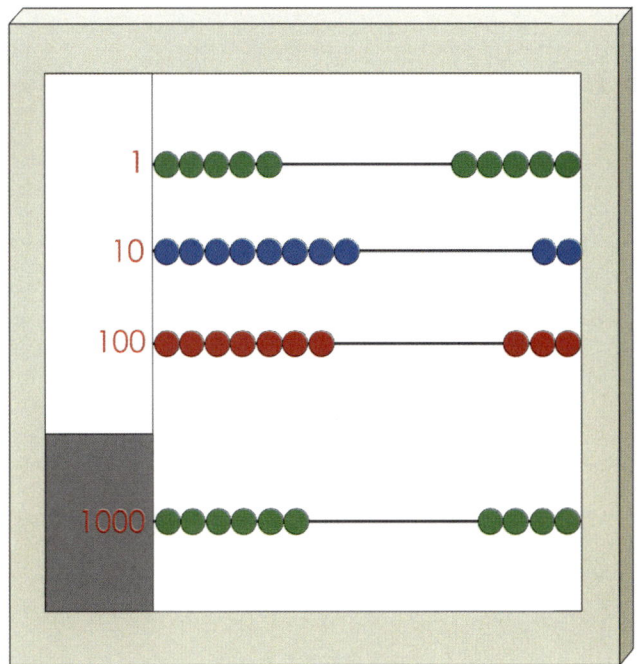

Hierarchy of Thousands	Simple Hierarchy		
U	H	T	U

2. Colour the quantities.

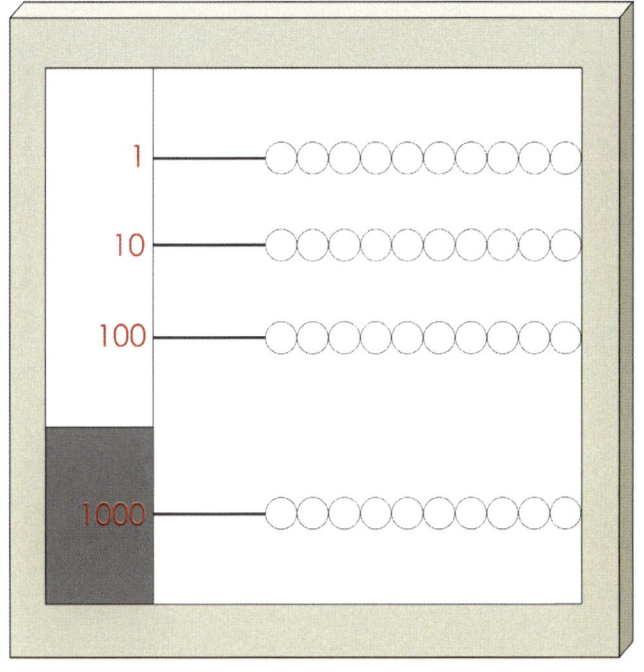

Hierarchy of Thousands	Simple Hierarchy		
U	H	T	U
6 ,	2	0	4

Page 11

Practice 1

Small Bead Frame
Introduction

1. Write the numbers.

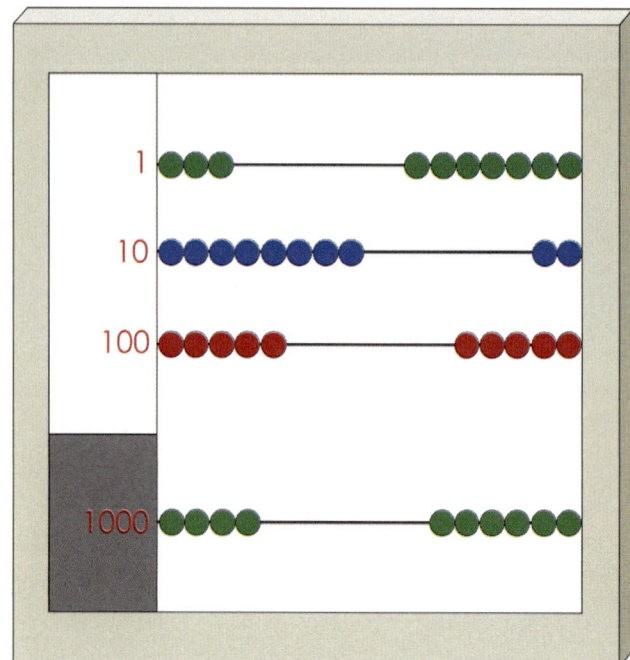

Hierarchy of Thousands	Simple Hierarchy		
U	H	T	U

2. Colour the quantities.

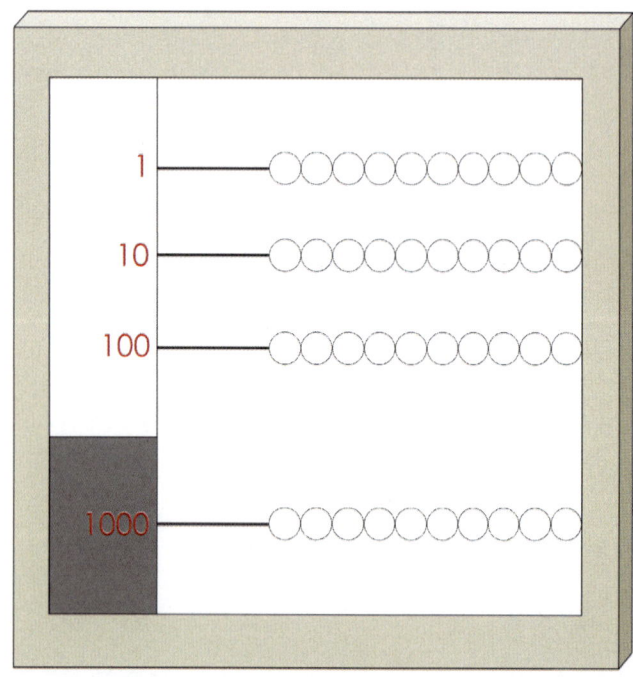

Hierarchy of Thousands	Simple Hierarchy		
U	H	T	U
3	5	8	7

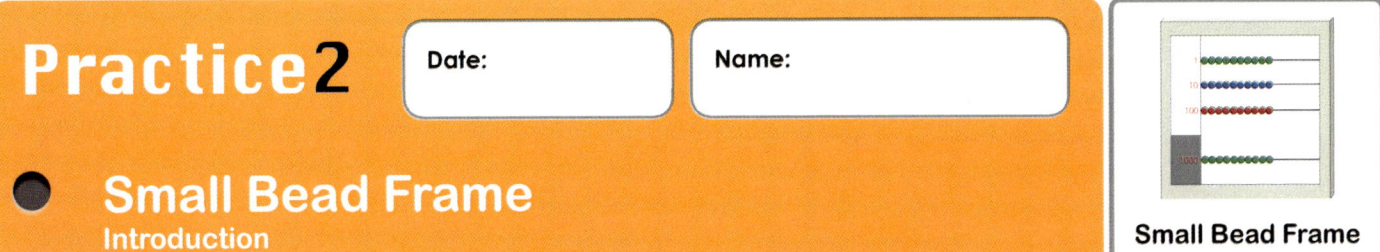

Practice 2

Small Bead Frame
Introduction

Small Bead Frame

1. Write the numbers.

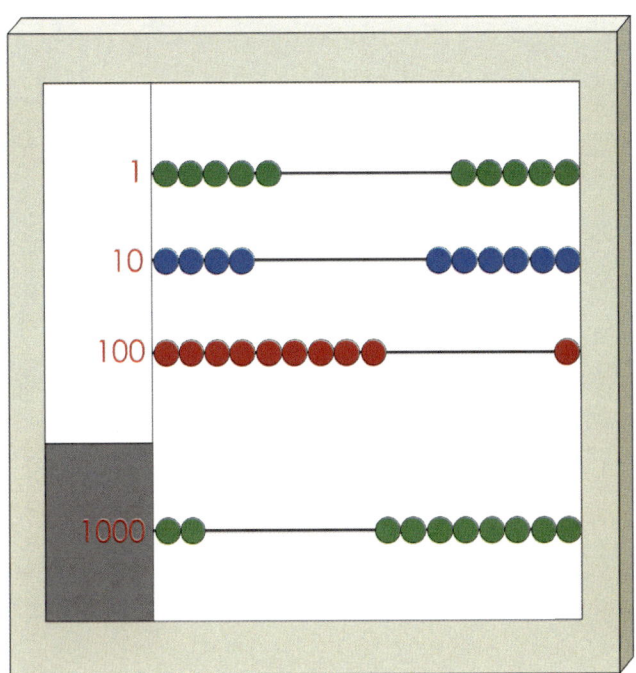

Hierarchy of Thousands	Simple Hierarchy		
U	H	T	U

2. Colour the quantities.

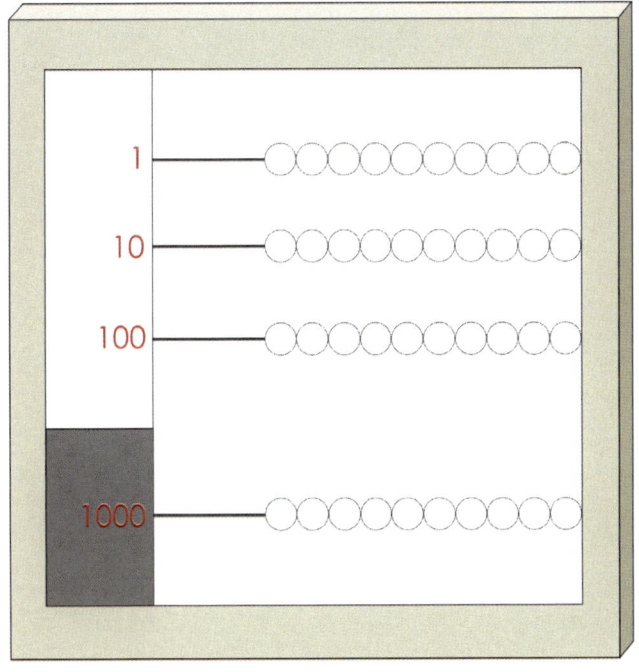

Hierarchy of Thousands	Simple Hierarchy		
U	H	T	U
9 ,	2	6	1

Page 13

Practice 3

Small Bead Frame
Introduction

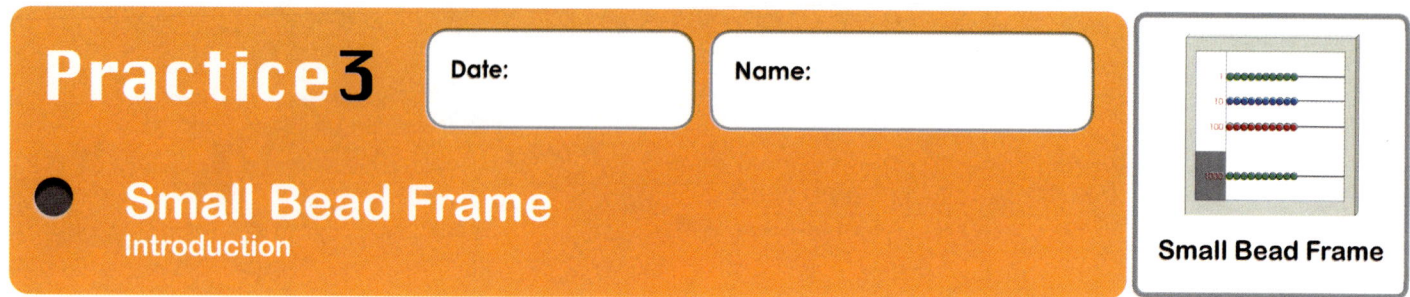

Small Bead Frame

1. Write the numbers.

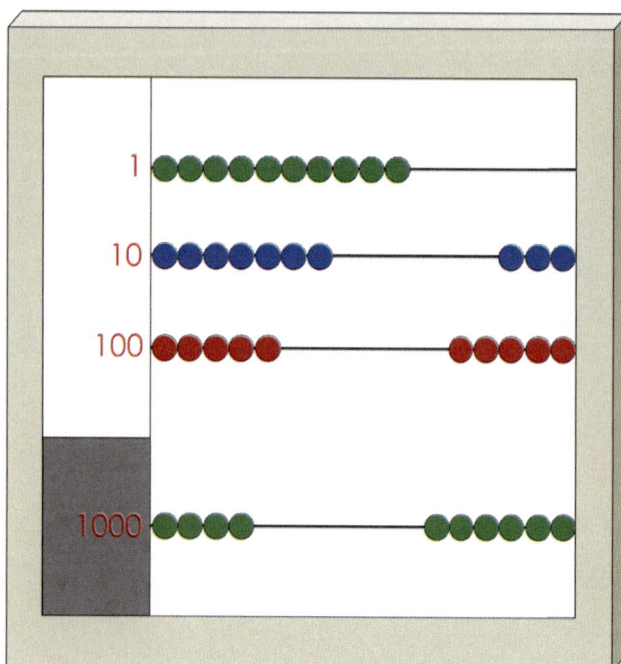

Hierarchy of Thousands	Simple Hierarchy		
U	H	T	U

2. Colour the quantities.

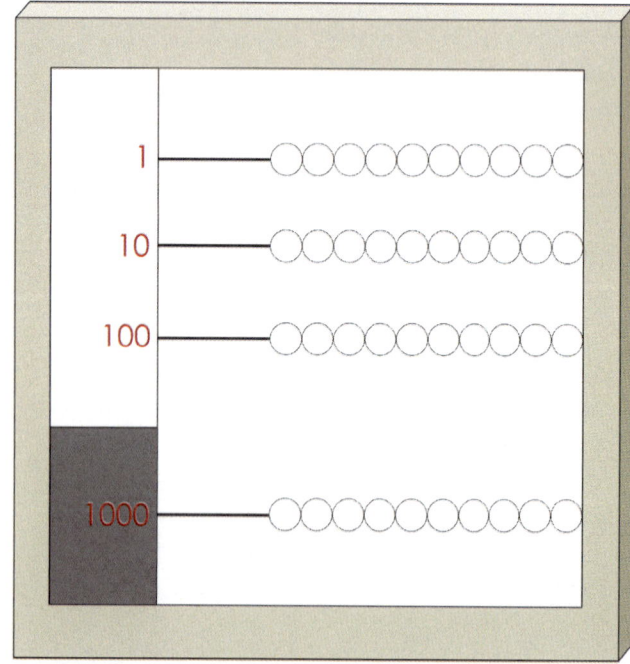

Hierarchy of Thousands	Simple Hierarchy		
U	H	T	U
8	4	5	0

Practice 4

Small Bead Frame
Introduction

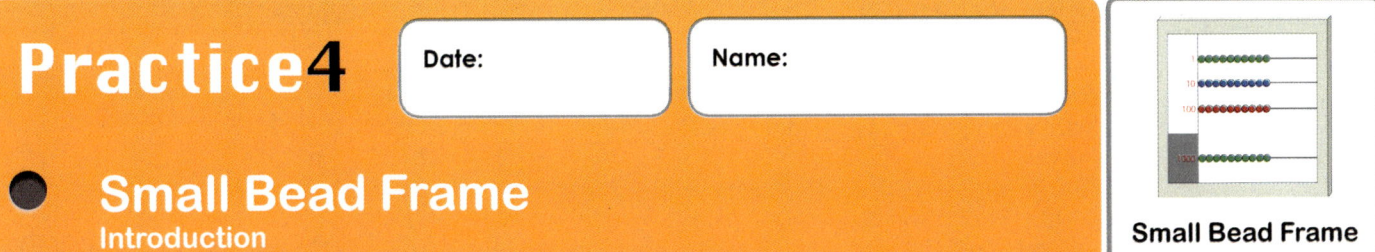

Small Bead Frame

1. Write the numbers.

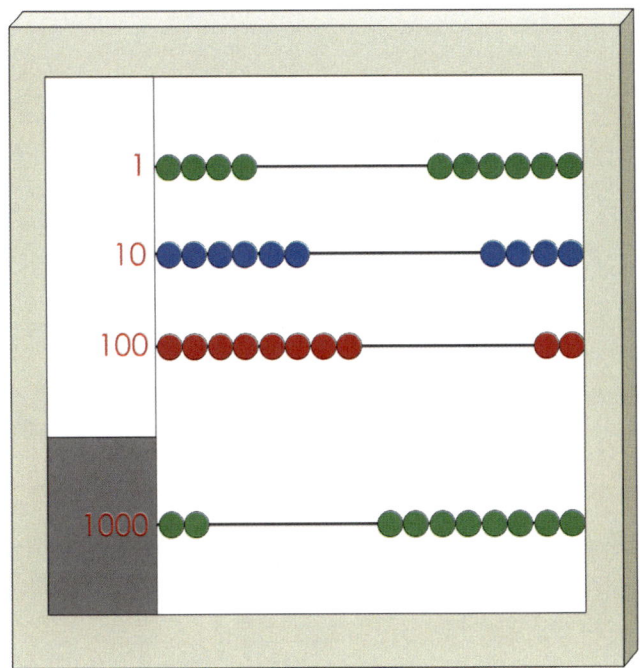

Hierarchy of Thousands	Simple Hierarchy		
U	H	T	U

2. Colour the quantities.

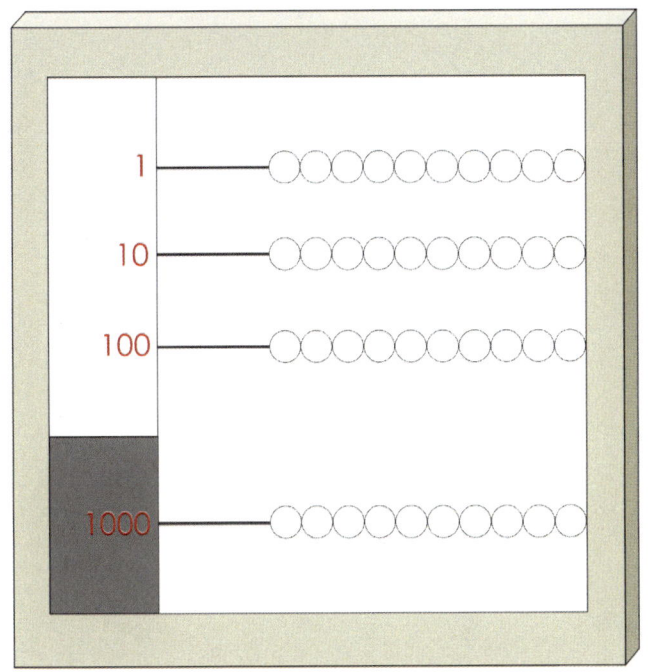

Hierarchy of Thousands	Simple Hierarchy		
U	H	T	U
4 ,	5	7	3

Page 15

Check-in
Small Bead Frame
Introduction

Small Bead Frame

1. Write the numbers.

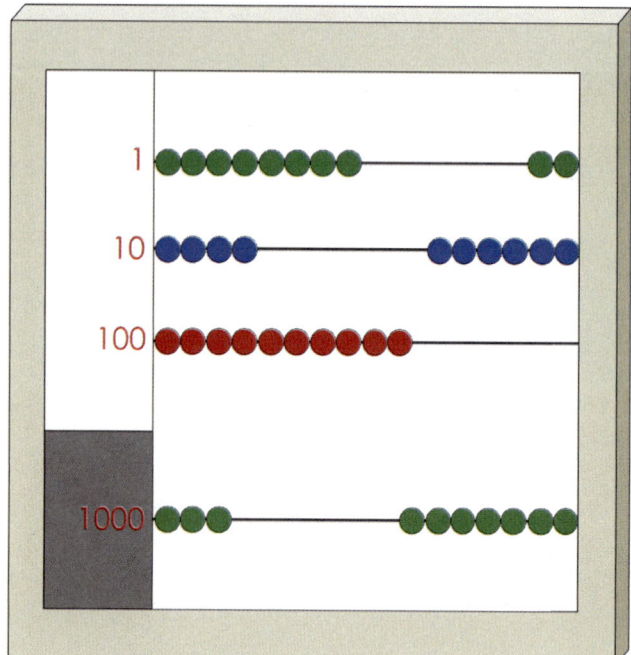

Hierarchy of Thousands	Simple Hierarchy	
U	H	T	U

2. Colour the quantities.

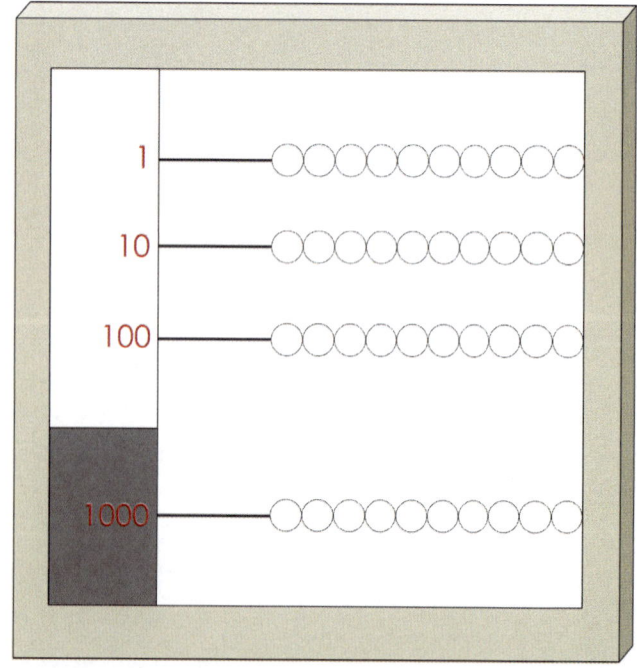

Hierarchy of Thousands	Simple Hierarchy	
U	H	T	U
4 ,	8	0	3

Meowntessori Montessori
Printable Materials / Workbooks / Worksheets

Small Bead Frame

Static Addition

Workbook

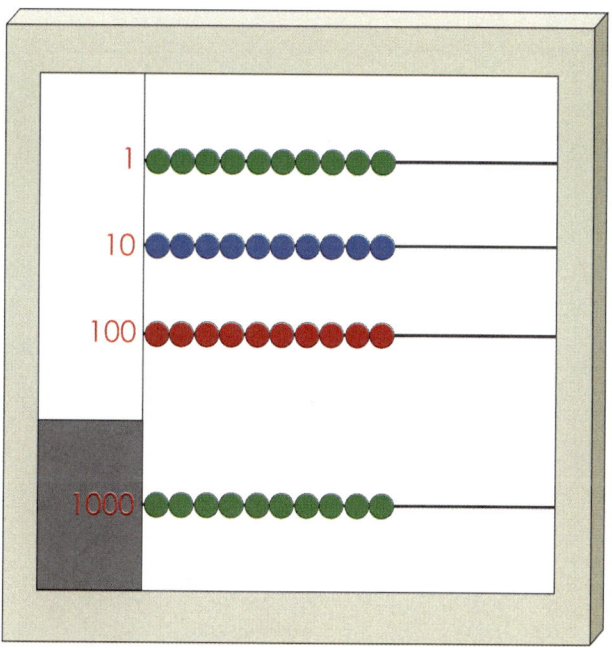

www.meowntessori.com
© Meowntessori Montessori All Rights Reserved

How to work

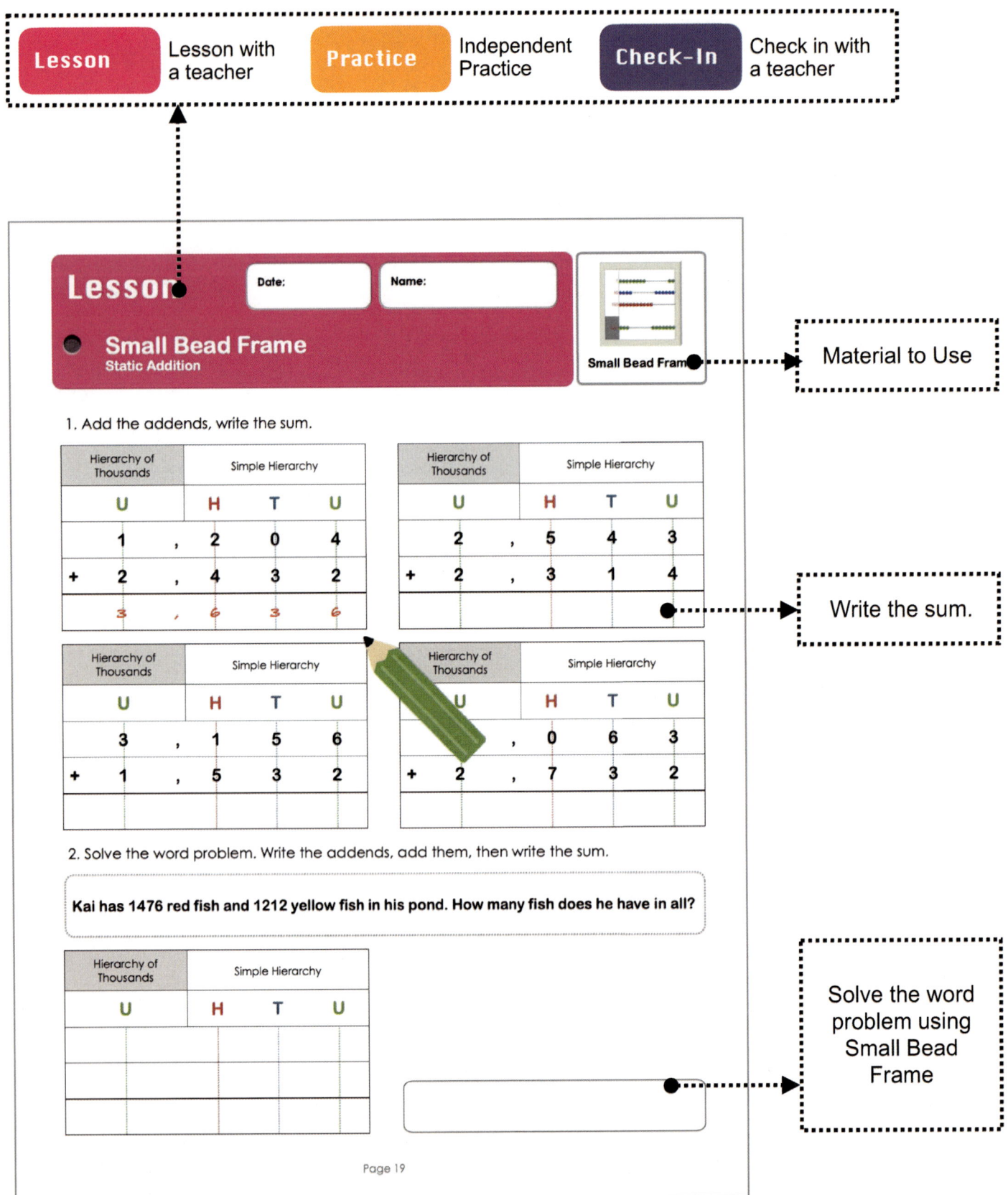

Lesson

Small Bead Frame
Static Addition

Small Bead Frame

1. Add the addends, write the sum.

Hierarchy of Thousands	Simple Hierarchy		
U	H	T	U
1,	2	0	4
+ 2,	4	3	2

Hierarchy of Thousands	Simple Hierarchy		
U	H	T	U
2,	5	4	3
+ 2,	3	1	4

Hierarchy of Thousands	Simple Hierarchy		
U	H	T	U
3,	1	5	6
+ 1,	5	3	2

Hierarchy of Thousands	Simple Hierarchy		
U	H	T	U
4,	0	6	3
+ 2,	7	3	2

2. Solve the word problem. Write the addends, add them, then write the sum.

Kai has 1476 red fish and 1212 yellow fish in his pond. How many fish does he have in all?

Hierarchy of Thousands	Simple Hierarchy		
U	H	T	U

Page 19

Practice 1

Date: Name:

Small Bead Frame
Static Addition

Small Bead Frame

1. Add the addends, write the sum.

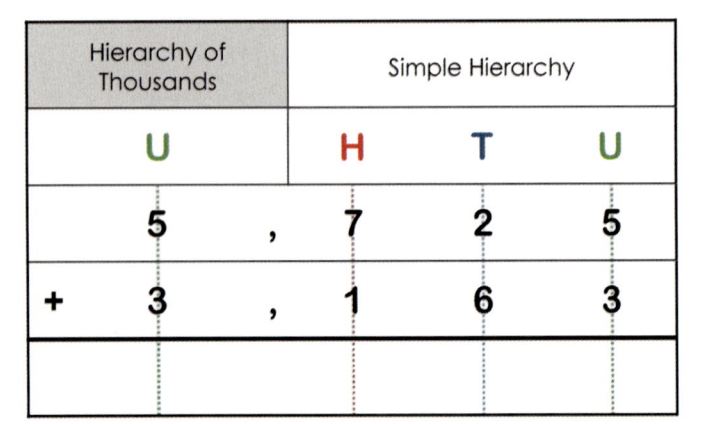

Hierarchy of Thousands	Simple Hierarchy		
U	H	T	U
5,	7	2	5
+ 3,	1	6	3

Hierarchy of Thousands	Simple Hierarchy		
U	H	T	U
6,	1	0	3
+ 1,	4	7	5

Hierarchy of Thousands	Simple Hierarchy		
U	H	T	U
7,	3	2	6
+ 2,	2	5	1

Hierarchy of Thousands	Simple Hierarchy		
U	H	T	U
8,	1	8	0
+ 1,	6	1	5

2. Solve the word problem. Write the addends, add them, then write the sum.

There are 1403 boys and 1571 girls in the school. How many children are there in the school?

Hierarchy of Thousands	Simple Hierarchy		
U	H	T	U

Practice 2

Date: **Name:**

Small Bead Frame
Static Addition

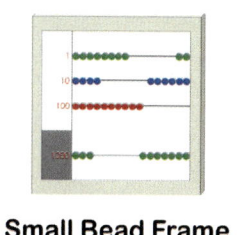

Small Bead Frame

1. Add the addends, write the sum.

Hierarchy of Thousands	Simple Hierarchy		
U	H	T	U
9 ,	3	1	2
+	4	3	2

Hierarchy of Thousands	Simple Hierarchy		
U	H	T	U
	5	3	4
+ 2 ,	1	4	5

Hierarchy of Thousands	Simple Hierarchy		
U	H	T	U
4 ,	5	1	2
+	1	8	3

Hierarchy of Thousands	Simple Hierarchy		
U	H	T	U
	1	4	1
+ 4 ,	6	2	5

2. Solve the word problem. Write the addends, add them, then write the sum.

Mark earned 2350 dollars last month. This month, he earned 1244 dollars. How much did he earn in total?

Hierarchy of Thousands	Simple Hierarchy		
U	H	T	U

Page 21

Practice 3

Small Bead Frame
Static Addition

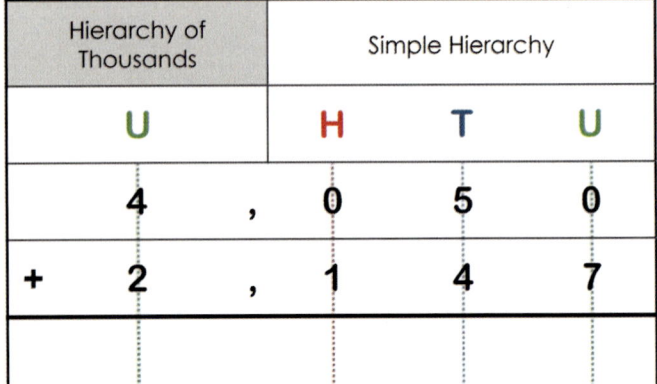

Small Bead Frame

1. Add the addends, write the sum.

Hierarchy of Thousands	Simple Hierarchy		
U	H	T	U
4 ,	0	5	0
+ 2 ,	1	4	7

Hierarchy of Thousands	Simple Hierarchy		
U	H	T	U
3 ,	5	6	9
+ 1 ,	0	2	0

Hierarchy of Thousands	Simple Hierarchy		
U	H	T	U
5 ,	0	0	0
+ 1 ,	0	0	0

Hierarchy of Thousands	Simple Hierarchy		
U	H	T	U
1 ,	3	5	7
+ 1 ,	8	7	5

2. Solve the word problem. Write the addends, add them, then write the sum.

> Ella walked 1643 steps yesterday, and 2211 steps today. How many steps did Ella walked in total?

Hierarchy of Thousands	Simple Hierarchy		
U	H	T	U

Page 22

Practice 4

Small Bead Frame
Static Addition

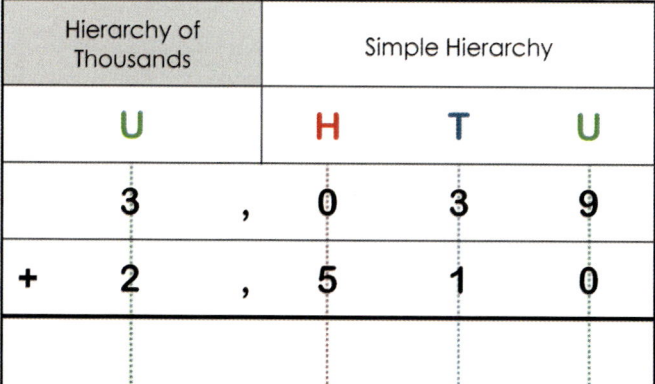

Small Bead Frame

1. Add the addends, write the sum.

Hierarchy of Thousands	Simple Hierarchy		
U	H	T	U
3 ,	0	3	9
+ 2 ,	5	1	0

Hierarchy of Thousands	Simple Hierarchy		
U	H	T	U
2 ,	4	4	7
+ 1 ,	3	4	2

Hierarchy of Thousands	Simple Hierarchy		
U	H	T	U
5 ,	3	7	5
+ 1 ,	2	1	3

Hierarchy of Thousands	Simple Hierarchy		
U	H	T	U
5 ,	6	0	1
+ 2 ,	1	6	5

2. Solve the word problem. Write the addends, add them, then write the sum.

Julie folded 1145 paper cranes, and Mike folded 1043 paper cranes this year. How many paper cranes did they fold in total?

Hierarchy of Thousands	Simple Hierarchy		
U	H	T	U

Page 23

Check-in

Small Bead Frame
Static Addition

Small Bead Frame

1. Add the addends, write the sum.

Hierarchy of Thousands	Simple Hierarchy		
U	H	T	U
3 ,	1	2	0
+	5	4	1

Hierarchy of Thousands	Simple Hierarchy		
U	H	T	U
2 ,	5	3	1
+ 1 ,	4	1	8

Hierarchy of Thousands	Simple Hierarchy		
U	H	T	U
3 ,	0	5	6
+	9	2	1

Hierarchy of Thousands	Simple Hierarchy		
U	H	T	U
4 ,	2	1	3
+ 4 ,	7	5	3

2. Solve the word problem. Write the addends, add them, then write the sum.

The store owner has 1453 grams of red apples and 1231 grams of green apples. How much do all of these apples weigh together?

Hierarchy of Thousands	Simple Hierarchy		
U	H	T	U

Meowntessori Montessori
Printable Materials / Workbooks / Worksheets

Small Bead Frame
Dynamic Addition
Workbook

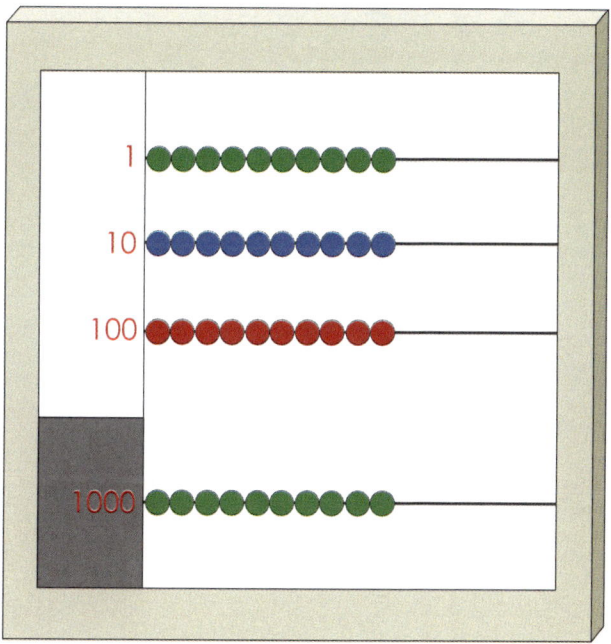

www.meowntessori.com

© Meowntessori Montessori All Rights Reserved

How to work

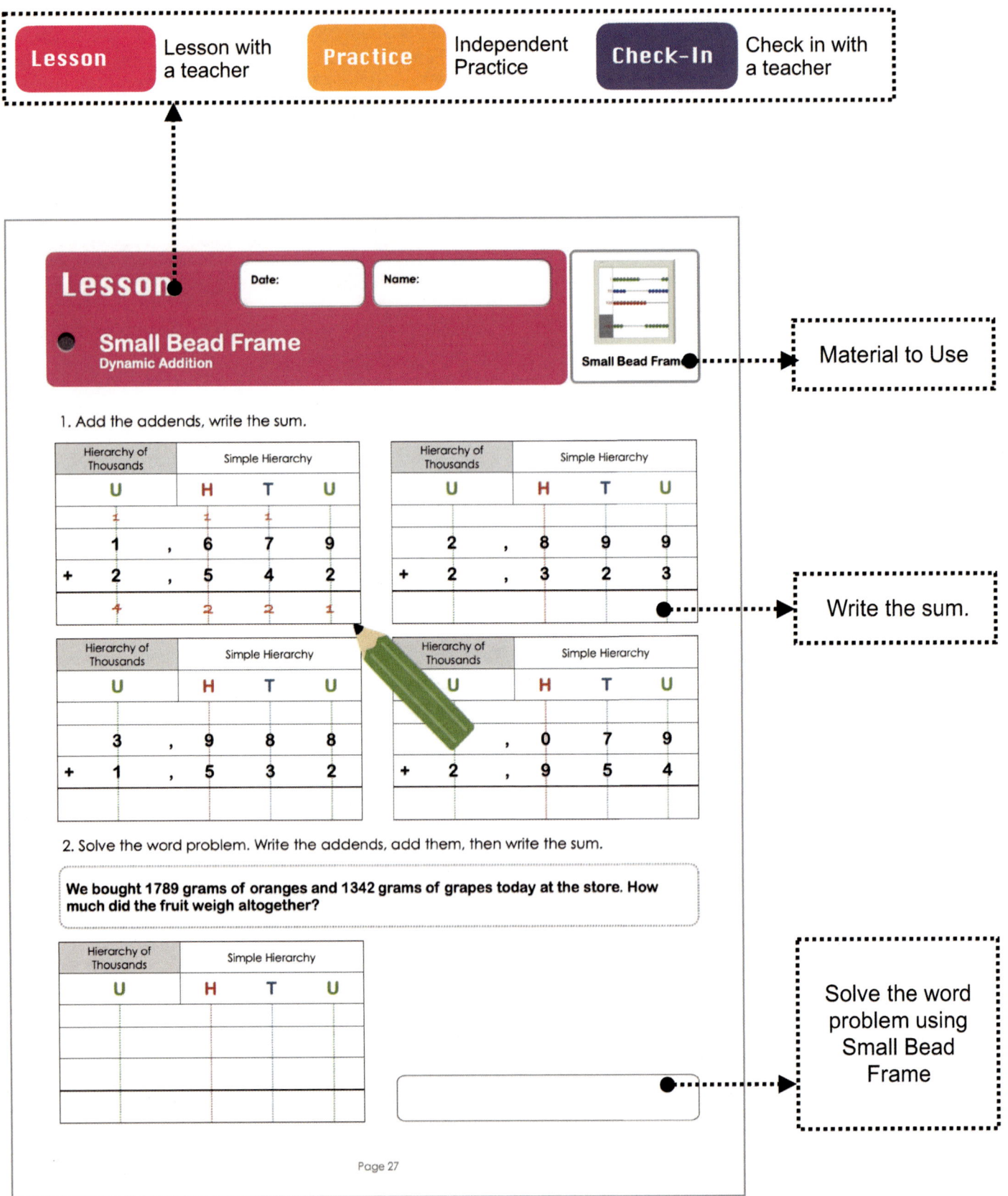

Lesson

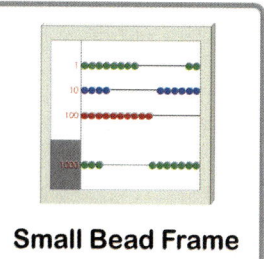

Small Bead Frame
Dynamic Addition

1. Add the addends, write the sum.

Hierarchy of Thousands	Simple Hierarchy		
U	H	T	U
1 ,	6	7	9
+ 2 ,	5	4	2

Hierarchy of Thousands	Simple Hierarchy		
U	H	T	U
2 ,	8	9	9
+ 2 ,	3	2	3

Hierarchy of Thousands	Simple Hierarchy		
U	H	T	U
3 ,	9	8	8
+ 1 ,	5	3	2

Hierarchy of Thousands	Simple Hierarchy		
U	H	T	U
4 ,	0	7	9
+ 2 ,	9	5	4

2. Solve the word problem. Write the addends, add them, then write the sum.

We bought 1789 grams of oranges and 1342 grams of grapes today at the store. How much did the fruit weigh altogether?

Hierarchy of Thousands	Simple Hierarchy		
U	H	T	U

Practice 1

Date: Name:

Small Bead Frame
Dynamic Addition

Small Bead Frame

1. Add the addends, write the sum.

Hierarchy of Thousands	Simple Hierarchy		
U	H	T	U
1 ,	7	8	9
+ 2 ,	4	3	2

Hierarchy of Thousands	Simple Hierarchy		
U	H	T	U
2 ,	6	8	7
+ 2 ,	4	3	4

Hierarchy of Thousands	Simple Hierarchy		
U	H	T	U
3 ,	7	6	8
+ 1 ,	4	4	3

Hierarchy of Thousands	Simple Hierarchy		
U	H	T	U
4 ,	6	7	5
+ 2 ,	5	3	6

2. Solve the word problem. Write the addends, add them, then write the sum.

> Sarah is carrying books for her school's book fair. She has 1598 picture books and 1634 chapter books. How many books does she have in total?

Hierarchy of Thousands	Simple Hierarchy		
U	H	T	U

Page 28

Practice 2

Small Bead Frame
Dynamic Addition

1. Add the addends, write the sum.

Hierarchy of Thousands	Simple Hierarchy		
U	H	T	U
5 ,	4	7	9
+ 1 ,	8	4	1

Hierarchy of Thousands	Simple Hierarchy		
U	H	T	U
6 ,	7	8	9
+ 1 ,	5	1	1

Hierarchy of Thousands	Simple Hierarchy		
U	H	T	U
7 ,	7	8	9
+ 1 ,	2	1	1

Hierarchy of Thousands	Simple Hierarchy		
U	H	T	U
4 ,	0	6	7
+ 1 ,	9	5	4

2. Solve the word problem. Write the addends, add them, then write the sum.

Lora has roses in her garden. She cut 1763 roses yesterday. Today, she cut 1477 roses. How many roses did Lora cut in total?

Hierarchy of Thousands	Simple Hierarchy		
U	H	T	U

Practice 3

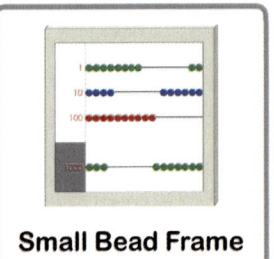

Small Bead Frame
Dynamic Addition

Small Bead Frame

1. Add the addends, write the sum.

Hierarchy of Thousands	Simple Hierarchy		
U	H	T	U
2 ,	3	4	5
+ 1 ,	8	7	6

Hierarchy of Thousands	Simple Hierarchy		
U	H	T	U
1 ,	5	3	4
+ 2 ,	5	7	6

Hierarchy of Thousands	Simple Hierarchy		
U	H	T	U
4 ,	5	1	2
+ 1 ,	7	9	8

Hierarchy of Thousands	Simple Hierarchy		
U	H	T	U
3 ,	2	4	1
+ 3 ,	8	7	9

2. Solve the word problem. Write the addends, add them, then write the sum.

> Pam donated 1683 socks, and Henry donated 1578 socks to help people. How many socks did they donate all together?

Hierarchy of Thousands	Simple Hierarchy		
U	H	T	U

Page 30

Practice 4

Date: Name:

Small Bead Frame
Dynamic Addition

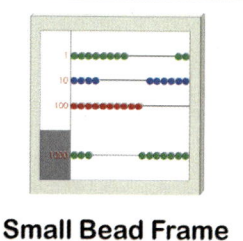

Small Bead Frame

1. Add the addends, write the sum.

Hierarchy of Thousands	Simple Hierarchy		
U	H	T	U
4,	0	0	3
+ 2,	9	9	9

Hierarchy of Thousands	Simple Hierarchy		
U	H	T	U
3,	2	4	5
+ 1,	8	9	8

Hierarchy of Thousands	Simple Hierarchy		
U	H	T	U
1,	1	1	1
+ 1,	9	9	9

Hierarchy of Thousands	Simple Hierarchy		
U	H	T	U
1,	9	9	9
+ 1,	1	1	1

2. Solve the word problem. Write the addends, add them, then write the sum.

Bill's classroom used 1762 pencil crayons. Peter's classroom used 2458 pencil crayons. How many crayons did they use in total?

Hierarchy of Thousands	Simple Hierarchy		
U	H	T	U

Page 31

Check-in

Date: Name:

Small Bead Frame
Dynamic Addition

Small Bead Frame

1. Add the addends, write the sum.

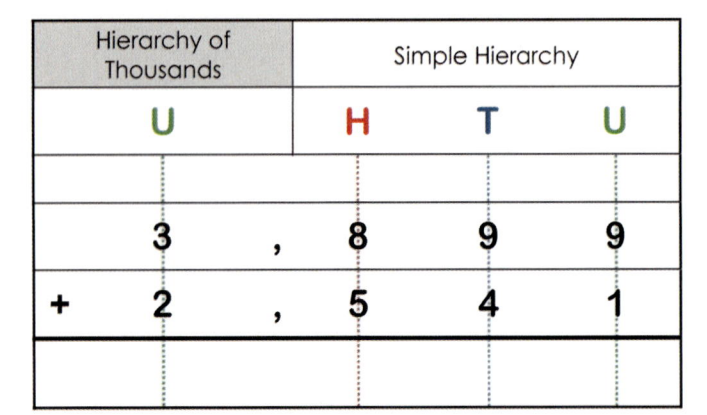

Hierarchy of Thousands	Simple Hierarchy		
U	H	T	U
3 ,	8	9	9
+ 2 ,	5	4	1

Hierarchy of Thousands	Simple Hierarchy		
U	H	T	U
2 ,	6	7	8
+ 1 ,	4	5	3

Hierarchy of Thousands	Simple Hierarchy		
U	H	T	U
3 ,	0	5	6
+	9	6	5

Hierarchy of Thousands	Simple Hierarchy		
U	H	T	U
1 ,	2	1	3
+ 4 ,	8	9	7

2. Solve the word problem. Write the addends, add them, then write the sum.

There were 1735 fish in the pond yesterday. Today, somebody added 1486 fish in the pond. How many fish does the pond have in total?

Hierarchy of Thousands	Simple Hierarchy		
U	H	T	U

Copyright © 2021 by Ayako Thiessen (Meowntessori Montessori)

All rights reserved. No part of this book may be reproduced in any form on by any electronic or mechanical means, including information storage and retrieval systems, without permission in writing from the publisher, except by reviewers, who may quote brief passages in a review.

ISBN: 9798654017413 (Paperback Edition)

Some characters and events in this book are fictitious. Any similarity to real persons, living or dead, is coincidental and not intended by the author.

Front Cover Image by Ayako Thiessen
Book Design by Ayako Thiessen

Printed by Amazon.com Inc., in Canada. (Independently Published)

First Printing Edition in 2020. (Edited in 2021)

Meowntessori Montessori
info@meowntessori.com
www.meowntessori.com

Made in the USA
Las Vegas, NV
11 September 2021